Spiralizer Recipe Book: Ultimate Beginners guide to Vegetable Pasta Spiralizer: Top Spiralizer Recipes For Weight loss, Gluten-free, Paleo, Low Carb & Holiday to Help You Lose Weight & Feel great- for Paderno, Veggetti & Spaghetti Shredders

by Laura Hill

Disclaimer:

The information provided in this book is designed to provide helpful information on the subjects discussed. The publisher and author are not responsible for any specific health or allergy needs that may require medical supervision and are not liable for any damages or negative consequences from any treatment, action, application or preparation, to any person reading or following the information in this book.

Table of Contents

Introduction

Spiralizing vegetables is one of the best ways to eat pasta meals which are low in calories and high in nutrients. While many people think they are only a means to make fancy, vegan meals, there is more to them than meets the eye. One thing which you have to keep in mind is the fact that you cannot start making spiral vegetables without the help of vegetable spiralizer. A vegetable spiralizer is a machine specifically designed to cut vegetables up in a circular manner which produces spiral shaped vegetable bits. While many people believe that spiralizing vegetables is a fad, there are actually certain benefits it offers.

Why is Veggettie better than Spaghetti?

Apart from being completely vegan, veggettie is perfect for people who want to incorporate a gluten-free, low-fat, nutritional diet without having to adhere to boring food items. Gone are the days when diets used to be dry, unappetizing meals.

With the help of spiralized vegetables, you can easily substitute pasta with a delicious, healthy alternative. Many people who are unable to handle the gluten in pasta dough often have to miss out on spaghettis and pastas too. Just because their body can't process it doesn't mean they don't want to eat it either.

If you or your loved ones have had to skip out on Italian meals because of this, you can whip up a nice, healthy, gluten surprise which allows them to keep eating spaghetti Bolognese and other tasty dishes they had to skip out on previously.

When you take the time to look at it, veggettie is actually healthier, gluten free and lower calorie than spaghetti. Even when cooked with other ingredients and topped with different toppings and sauces, veggettie still offers lower amounts of calories as compared to the dough spaghetti and pasta dishes.

Which Vegetables Can Be Spiralized?

Before you begin to spiralize, you need to know which vegetables can be spiralized successfully. Owing to their shapes, you can only use those vegetables which are bigger in length and width.

Because of this factor, you have a limited number of vegetables to choose from but they can be just as delicious in any meal. Among them, the following are the most popularly used to create various veggettie and spiralized vegetable dishes with ease:

Zucchini

With their straight, long bodies, Zucchinis are perfect for making veggettie. They are the most popularly spiralized vegetables mainly because they are so easy to find, easy to use and the resulting veggettie is always close to spaghetti in texture. They are also extremely easy to cook which also makes them popular to eat and use. You can even eat them raw.

Cucumbers

Similar to Zucchini in texture, cucumbers are rich in water and are not as widely used. However, if they are drained properly, they can produce a crunchy spiral which is delicious and refreshing to have on hot days.

Moreover, the neutral taste of cucumbers makes them easy to pair with other items in a salad or dish and can be eaten raw too.

Beets

Red beets are high in nutrition and are also pleasant to have as spiralized veggettie. Moreover, their dark color makes them look appealing in salads. Red beets should be thoroughly washed in order to get rid of the red juice and color they release. While washing it will not make the color go away, it can reduce the amount of red juice it has. You can eat them raw too.

Butternut Squashes

Creamy, buttery and extremely healthy for you, butternut squashes actually make great vegetables to use in spiraling and to make veggettie from. Moreover, they can be cooked, blanched, boiled and incorporated in more ways than one. Eating them raw is not really recommended.

Eggplants

Not popularly used but when they are in season, give these a try. Eggplants are also the perfect shape for using in a spiralizing machine and can produce nice long strands of veggettie. Moreover, they have great texture too but they have to be cooked carefully as they can have a rubbery texture if you overcook them. Don't try and eat them raw.

Carrots

Similar to cucumbers in popularity, carrots can be a little challenging to spiralize. You will have to prep them more carefully because carrots can be oddly shaped, making it harder to get long strings of veggettie. However, they can be easily eaten raw and are perfect for salads and cold meals.

Sweet Potatoes and Potatoes

Both have similar textures although sweet potatoes can be orange toned and sweeter in taste. They are also easy to cook and have as a side. Spiralizing them can also produce good quality veggettie which is tasty and has good length to it too. These are better when cooked so avoid eating them raw.

Jicama

Almost like a turnip in texture, the Jicama is slightly sweet in flavor. It can be a bit difficult to find but can be used to make great veggettie. Since Jicama is also smaller, it can be harder to get a good amount of noodles from it. Nonetheless, the flavor of the Jicama is well worth the effort it takes to make them.

How to Use the Vegetable Spiralizer Efficiently

Now you know which vegetables you can use for spiralizing and how the spiralizer is better for you and your family, you will have to get your hands on a spiralizing machine. The machine is the most efficient way for you to get the noodles you want out of the vegetable and minimize wastage.

Many people prefer to use a julienne peeler but it can be time consuming and tiring to get vegetables cut into uniform noodle like strands. Cut down the work by investing in a spiralizing machine. You won't regret it.

Even when you have the machine, you have to make sure to use it efficiently in order to minimize wastage and maximize how much the vegetable or fruit yields. For this purpose, you need to pay attention to the following:

Prepping Vegetables and Fruits

Before you start spiralizing your vegetables and fruits, take the time to prep them a little in order to ensure proper spiralization in the spiralizer. All fruits and vegetables should be peeled, unless you want them to have an extra crunch. However, cooking the noodles with peels on often gives them a weird texture because of the peeled and un-peeled edges.

For a more even cook, peel the vegetable or fruit you are using. Moreover, if the peel is inedible, go ahead and remove it. Cut all vegetables down to size, ensuring the piece you use is at least 1.5 inches wide.

Regardless of the kind of vegetable or fruit you are using, cut their ends on both sides, pop them into the spiralizer and get a bowl full of veggettie! You might also want to core out fruits like apples in order to remove the pip they contain.

Once you have the vegetable or fruit prepared, attach it to the spiralizer by pushing the largest area of the vegetable on to the round knob. Once that is attached, push the prickly press on to the other part, making sure the vegetable is securely sandwiched between both ends. Then all you have to do is turn the handle and get some easy veggettie.

Using Different Blades

Depending on the kind of spiralizer you got your hands on, you can have the option of using three or four different blade settings. In the eBook, we will simply refer to them as Blade A, Blade B and Blade C.

Using Blade A will produce thin strands of veggettie which will be similar to spaghetti in size. However, they may be longer, based on the length of the vegetable they were extracted from. Blade A is usually the most commonly used blade setting.

Blade B happens to be similar to Blade A. It produces long strands but they tend to be thicker and can be like bucatini pasta if you compare the thickness. If you don't like the thin strands you get, give this blade setting a try.

Blade C produces vegetables and fruits which are spiralized in a thinner and broader manner. The strands you get from them almost look like ribbons since they are thin and broad. They can be compared to papparadelle when you look at them.

With the help of these three blades, you can produce different kinds of veggettie, ensuring variety and diversity in your meals with ease.

Cleaning the Spiralizer

Once you have used the spiralizer, you have to clean it immediately. The main reason is because it is extremely unhygienic to leave the spiralizer as it is. Fruits and vegetables do have natural enzymes which need to be cleaned off with more than a simple rinse of water.

Moreover, the spiralizer has a plastic body which is white in color and can be stained, particularly if you are using beets. This is not going to come off easily and you could end up with a weirdly discolored machine. Nonetheless, cleaning a spiralizer might seem more confusing because of the blade settings and handles on it.

The best option is to get a round brush with which you can scrub the blades. Apply some cleaning soap on the brush and under running water, give the whole spiralizer a good scrub with the help of the brush. All spiralizers are easy to clean and waterproof so don't leave your spiralizer lying around once you use it. Clean it as soon as you are done with it.

Drying

Vegetables aren't meant to be eaten as noodles. Moreover, chopping them up is sure to make them release their juices. This could happen, particularly when you leave them to rest in a bowl while you get the remaining ingredients together for the dish. You should also consider the fact that vegetables like cucumber have a water content of almost 95%. That's a lot of moisture,

To avoid your vegetables turning soggy or to stop them from releasing too much water when you are cooking them, dry them gently with the help of tissue paper. Place a sheet of tissue paper with the spiralized vegetable on top of it. Add another sheet of tissue paper on top and then pat everything dry.

For cucumbers, you might have to repeat this step twice or thrice before you get the moisture out properly. Doing so beforehand ensures that you don't have excess water in your dishes or end up with soggy noodles which can be rather unappetizing in texture.

Cutting Noodles to Size

When you are spiralizing your vegetables, you will definitely come across noodles which are extremely long. While spaghetti is supposed to be long, these noodles can be longer than them. Therefore, to make it easier to eat and serve, remember to cut your noodles down to size before you start to cook them.

Some people choose to cook the noodles long and then break them as they are cooking but it could have you end up with uneven noodles which can be a trouble to eat. Cutting them before cooking can make it easier for everyone involved.

Vegetable Size Impacts Yield

The size of the vegetable you use can make a huge impact on the amount of noodles you get from it. Therefore, always make sure to pick produce which is at least medium-sized or large.

Small vegetables will also be more challenging in fixing to the spiralizer and you will end having to use the spiralizer twice as many times to get as much veggettie as you could have gotten from a medium-sized fruit or vegetable.

To get a more accurate measurement, take a toothbrush and compare its length with the vegetables you have. Whether you have a cucumber, zucchini or carrot, lay it down next to the toothbrush to make sure it is as big as or bigger than the toothbrush.

The circumference of the vegetable should be around 1.5 inches as something wider will end up yielding noodles which are too flat and do not have a spiral curve to them.

Now that you know how to make spiral veggettie with more efficiency, you can get to work spiralizing tons of different items.

On the other hand, how can you make quick and easy meals with the noodles you produce? Even the best planned meals can take you 45 minutes or so. Spiral vegetable noodles can also make you feel more confused. What exactly could you cook with it?

If you are confused, take a look at the following ways you can make quick and easy meals with the help of spiralizer. These 7 ways are not only easy, they are quick too and your meals will be ready in a matter of minutes.

1. Raw is Good

The best part about it is the fact that you really do not need to cook these noodles. If you have your noodles ready, just add them to the rest of the ingredients and serve with some nice vinaigrette on top.

The best part about going raw is that you don't have to wait a long time. You could easily be munching on a bowl of raw vegetable noodles within 30 seconds. Fresh vegetable noodles also pair well with hot and creamy sauces.

However, remember to dry them with some tissue paper first before you start to add them to the sauce. Otherwise, you might end up with an exceedingly runny sauce because the vegetables released their water.

2. Soups

Apart from eating them raw, you can also make exceptionally good soup which can taste amazing with a helping of vegetable noodles in them. The trick though is to add the noodles towards the end of the cook, allowing them to get blanched in the soup.

Apart from certain vegetables, cooking the noodles for long periods of time may result in mushy and broken noodles which don't taste much like good vegetables. Moreover, a soup is one of the easiest things to cook, literally requiring you to add all the ingredients into one pot and letting them brew away.

Just make a soup any way you like and remembering what we said earlier, just add a handful or two of the vegetable noodles towards the end of the cook and you will be more than happy with the end result.

3. Noodle Salad!

You can also choose to incorporate your veggettie into a salad to add an extra twist to your meal. When you think of vegetables, salads might pop up in your head as one of the most common ways to have vegetable noodles. Since they are so easy to pair up, you can introduce more ingredients like chicken, shrimp, bacon or other varieties.

Drizzle a nice, light sauce on top and you are good to go. When making salads for the first time, try to avoid using thicker sauces since they can mask the vegetables and make the salad too heavy. Light, tart, citrusy sauces work best in noodle salads but you might want to go with your own preference when it comes to this.

4. Simple Ingredients

Whether you are making a noodle salad, soup or a whole other dish, remember to pair the noodles with simple ingredients which are easy for you to cook and, most importantly; ingredients which you know how to use. When cooking anything for the first time, it is easy to feel intimidated or overwhelmed.

You don't want the dish going wrong and you want to get something which is at least yummy, even if it isn't right. With simple ingredients, you not only increase the chances of cooking something you like but if you get something wrong, you can correct them with ease.

By complicating everything with tougher ingredients or something you have never used before, you only add more pressure on yourself. Cook with things you know and then graduate on to tougher cooks.

5. No Sauce Cooks

Noodles just seem to be made for sauce but you can easily get bored of them too. What do you do to incorporate a little variety into your vegetables? Well, how about you only focus on seasoning them right and adding the right ingredients? Whether you make something with oregano, parmesan and prosciutto or an improvised version of some other dish, cook without the sauce and evolve your dish around it.

In the end, you will get a light filling meal. Cooking in this manner will also allow you to not only master your seasoning skills but also create noodle pasta which can be eaten as a snack, for breakfast or for lunch too. Eating light but eating right is one of the biggest secrets behind having a healthy diet.

6. Garnishing

Start figuring out garnishing which can complement the vegetable noodles you are using. This might seem easier than it actually is because your noodles are not exactly like the paste noodles. Pasta happens to be rather neutral in taste and you can easily pair them with any kind of cheese, sauce, herbs and what not.

On the other hand, vegetable noodles can have their own unique flavor profiles. The trick here is to find a way to use this flavor and find garnishes which amplify it or complement it. Garnishes which seem to clash with the flavors are definitely a no-no and should be avoided.

Even certain herbs might not be suited for your vegetable noodle dish so take some time to test and taste. Your personal preference might also influence the kind of garnishing which becomes a staple in your pantry for your veggettie dishes.

7. Mix and Match

While you might have your own preference for the kind of veggettie you want, you actually get to take advantage of three different blade settings which can help to get three different kinds of vegetable pasta. When you have this kind of freedom, what are you waiting for? Start switching the blades around and mix and match different veggettie to create fun dishes.

You can even make salads, soups, pasta dishes and more using two different kinds of veggettie made with the help of the spiralizer. Moreover, certain types of veggettie are more suited for certain dishes. While the thin veggettie is a popular choice for many people, you may find that some dishes just taste better or are more fun to eat with the other versions. Mix and match and enjoy the variety your diet has.

Top 7 Gluten Free Recipes

One of the biggest reasons many people switch to all vegan or Paleo type diets is owing to the fact that they are gluten free. One of the main things they usually have to give up is dough pasta owing to its grain and gluten content.

If you are or anyone else around you is missing those long, swirly treats, then whip out the spiralizer and try out these gluten free recipes!

Asian Cucumber Salad with Spicy Ginger and Sesame Seeds

With this spicy salad, you can tantalize your taste buds and enjoy the tart combination of ginger, spice and cool Asian cucumbers too.

Nutritional Value per serving:
- Calories: 195

- Carbohydrates: 38g

- Fat: 3.2g

- Saturated Fat: 0.1g

- Protein: 8.3g

- Fiber: 6.2g

Preparation Time: 15 minutes
Cooking Time: 10 minutes

This makes 2 to 4 servings. Increase measurements by multiplying them with the number of servings in mind to make more.

Ingredients for the Salad
- 2 cucumbers (medium sized, Blade C)

- 1 tablespoon of jalapeno peppers (minced finely)

- ¼ cup of onions (red, sliced thinly)

- 1 tablespoon of sesame seeds (toasted)

- 2 tablespoons of cilantro (fresh, chopped roughly)

- Sea salt (fine, according to preference)

For the Ginger Sesame Vinaigrette
- 2 tablespoons of sesame oil (dark)

- 1 tablespoon of olive oil (extra virgin)

- 1 tablespoon of soy sauce (gluten free)

- 2 tablespoons of vinegar (rice wine)

- 2 teaspoons of honey (raw, organic)

- 2 teaspoons of ginger (fresh, minced)

- 1 clove of garlic (fresh, minced)

- Red chili flakes (according to preference

Method:
Take a colander and place all the cucumber ribbons inside it. Season with sea salt, toss them well to coat them well and leave them in the colander to drain properly.
In a small bowl, combine the sesame oil, olive oil, soy sauce, vinegar, honey, ginger, garlic and chili flakes and mix well to completely combine the ingredients. Taste and adjust seasoning if required.
Now take the cucumbers out of the colander and rinse the salt off them. Using tissues, pat them dry. Take a large bowl and combine the cucumbers, jalapenos and onions. Only add half of the cilantro and the sesame seeds. Now add the dressing you prepared to the bowl. Mix gently and make sure everything is combined well.

Serve:
Serve cold. Sprinkle the remaining sesame seeds and cilantro on top of the salad as a garnish.

Creamy Cheese Sauce with Beet Veggettie

Made with goat cheese, this creamy sauce and beet veggettie salad will become a family favorite in no time at all. This is also a fun way of getting your kids to eat beet too. You can use any kind of beets, red or yellow to make veggettie for this recipe.

Nutritional Value per serving:
- Calories: 130

- Carbohydrates: 16g

- Fat: 3.2g

- Saturated Fat: 0.1g

- Protein: 8.3g

- Fiber: 6.2g

Preparation Time: 15 minutes
Cooking Time: 5 minutes

This makes 2 to 4 servings. Increase measurements by multiplying them with the number of servings in mind to make more.

Ingredients for the Salad
- 6 beets (red or yellow, medium sized, Blade A or B)

- ¾ cups of cashews (pre-soaked for at least 2 hours)

- ¾ cup of water

- 1 bunch of chives (chopped roughly)

- 2 shallots

- ¼ cup of cilantro (fresh)

- ¾ cup of goat's cheese (fresh, crumbled)

- · 1 clove of garlic

- · 4 tablespoons of sunflower seeds (toasted)

- · Salt and Pepper (according to taste)

Method:

Take a large pot and fill it with water. Let it come to the boil before adding enough salt to make the water taste exceptionally salty. Once it becomes salty, take the beet veggettie you prepared and add it to the pot.

Let it cook for three minutes or until it comes to the boil. The veggettie should be soft and slightly al dente. Once it has the right texture, drain, and allow it to rest in a colander to get all the water out.

In a blender, combine the cashews, chives, cilantro, goat cheese, garlic, salt, pepper and water. Add the water slowly and stop to scrape the sides of the blender with a spoon to combine all the ingredients properly. Blend until you get a smooth sauce. Taste and adjust seasoning if required.

Now take a large pot and combine the veggettie with the sauce.

Mix well and reheat the veggettie on low medium heat in order to combine it with the sauce more easily. Add 3 tablespoons of sunflower seeds now, give it a good stir and serve.

Serve:

Serve warm. Serve each helping with some sunflower seeds, cilantro and goat cheese crumbled on top.

BBQ Shrimps and Basil, Avocado and Zucchini Noodles with Corn

The delicious roast corn and basil and avocado sauce will make these zucchini noodles truly shine. The BBQ shrimps help to make this dish truly mouthwatering.

Nutritional Value per serving:
- Calories: 325.5

- Carbohydrates: 34.1g

- Fat: 16.9g

- Protein: 14.3g

Preparation Time: 7 minutes
Cooking Time: 5 minutes

This makes 2 servings. Increase measurements by multiplying them with the number of servings in mind to make more.

Ingredients for the Sauce
- 5 teaspoons of lime juice

- Sea salt grinder (8 Cranks)

- Peppercorn grinder (10 Cranks)

- 1 avocado

- ¼ cup of Greek yogurt

- 12 leaves of basil (fresh)

- 1 clove of garlic (medium, minced)

For the Veggettie
- 2 to 3 zucchinis (medium sized, Blade A or B)

- 8 shrimps (medium sized, cleaned, deveined)

- 1 lime (whole, fresh)

- 2 teaspoons of honey (raw, organic)

- 2 teaspoons of ginger (fresh, minced)

- 1 clove of garlic (fresh, minced)

- Olive Oil (for cooking)

- 1 corn cob

Method:

Set your oven to preheat at 400°. Meanwhile, take a baking tray and line with some baking paper. Take the corn cob, wash it and spray it with some olive oil and season with salt and pepper. Once the oven comes up to temperature, pop the kernels in and let them roast for 10 minutes. Scrape off the kernels, into a bowl and set aside once they are cooked.

In a blender, combine the lime juice, avocado, garlic, Greek yogurt, basil salt and pepper. Add the lime juice slowly and stop to scrape the sides of the blender with a spoon to combine all the ingredients properly. Blend until you get a smooth sauce. Taste and adjust seasoning if required.

In a separate bowl, combine the shrimps with chili powder, salt and pepper and mix to coat them well and set aside. Take a skillet and heat some olive oil on medium heat. Add the shrimps to the hot pan. Cut the lime and squeeze the juice on to the shrimps as they cook. Cook each shrimp for 2 to 3 minutes on each side or until they turn opaque and are cooked through.

Serve:

Serve warm. Serve each helping of noodles with a good dollop of sauce, roast corn and 4 shrimps added on top.

Cucumber Salad with Garlic Tahini Sauce

The cucumber ribbons produced with the spiralizer are not just pretty. This easy recipe will have you munching on something delicious and tasty in a matter of minutes.

Nutritional Value per serving:
- Calories: 320

- Carbohydrates: 12.1g

- Fat: 8.9g

- Protein: 7.1g

Preparation Time: 7 minutes
Cooking Time: 5 minutes
This makes 2 to 4 servings. Increase measurements by multiplying them with the number of servings in mind to make more.

Ingredients for the Sauce
- 2 tablespoons of Tahini paste (unsalted)

- 2 tablespoons of olive oil (extra virgin)

- 2 tablespoons of lemon juice (fresh)

- 3 cloves of garlic (small)

- 1 teaspoon of maple syrup

- Sea salt and Pepper (freshly ground)

For the Salad
- 1 cucumber (large. Use 2 if medium sized, Blade C)

- ¼ cup of red onions (sliced thinly)

- ¼ cup olives (kalamata, pitted, chopped roughly)

- ¼ cup of mint leaves (fresh, chopped roughly)

- Sesame seeds (according to preference, can use hemp seeds instead too)

Method:

Spiralize your cucumbers into ribbons and set them aside in a colander to drain all water from them. You can also dab them with tissues to get the water out faster.

While the cucumber is draining, combine the Tahini paste, olive oil, garlic, maple syrup, lemon juice and salt and pepper, with the help of a whisk. Mix until they are well combined. Taste and adjust seasoning if required.

Once the sauce is ready, check the cucumber ribbons and cut them down to size. Transfer them into a large bowl and add the mint and red onions to it. Add the dressing on top and toss everything well to coat them evenly in it.

Serve:
Serve as is with some chopped olives, mint and sesame seeds added on top.

Mouthwatering Zucchini Noodles with Scallops & Bacon

Bacon and scallop go hand in hand in this delicious recipe. The zucchini veggettie makes this dish exceedingly healthy and completely nutritious to have for lunch or dinner.

Nutrition Value:
For Noodles
- Calories: 33
- Carbohydrates: 6.1g
- Fiber: 2g

For Scallops and Bacon
- Calories: 190
- Cholesterol: 50mg
- Sodium: 550mg
- Carbohydrates: 2g
- Protein: 18g

Ingredients
- 1 lb petite cleaned and rinsed bay scallops
- 6 slices sugar free bacon
- 2 teaspoon garlic powder
- 6 green onions
- Fresh lemon juice
- Sea salt and black pepper
- For Pasta
- 8 medium zucchini

Equipment:
- Spiral slicer
- Flat bottom pan

Method:
- Prepare zucchini noodles as explained before. Set aside
- Dry the scallops with a clean dish towel or paper towel
- Cook the bacon in a large flat bottomed pan until crisp
- Once cooked. Remove from the pan and set aside.
- Pour off excess bacon fat and save for later. Use some of it to coat the pan lightly.

- Take a high sided pan and add about 2 teaspoon of bacon fat. Bring to medium high heat.
- Add the zucchini noodles and garlic powder. Season to taste with salt and pepper.
- Sauté the zucchini noodles until just softened
- Chop the cooked reserved bacon into pieces
- Remove the noodles from the heat and toss them with 2/3 of the bacon, the white parts of the chopped green onions (optional) and a squeeze of lemon juice.
- Place the flat bottomed pan on medium high heat. Add the dried scallops to the pan
- Sear the scallops until golden brown on the bottom. Flip over and sear for 1 - 2 minutes
- Remove the scallops from the heat and toss them in with the noodles
- Garnish noodles with the remaining bacon pieces and green onions. Enjoy!

Feta, Chicken and Spinach with Zucchini Noodles

Combining feta, chicken and baby spinach in this tasty dish is easy and healthy for you and your family. The light ingredients make this dish perfect as a snack or a light meal.

Nutritional Value per serving:
· Calories: 250

· Carbohydrates: 20g

· Fat: 3.2g

· Saturated Fat: 0.1g

· Protein: 10g

· Fiber: 6.2g

Preparation Time: 15 minutes
Cooking Time: 5 minutes

This makes 2 to 4 servings. Increase measurements by multiplying them with the number of servings in mind to make more.

Ingredients
· 2 to 3 chicken breasts (cubed, tenderloins)

· ½ teaspoon of garlic powder

· 1 cup of spinach

· 1 zucchini (large, Blade A or B)

· ¼ cup of feta cheese (cubed)

· Lemon juice from half a lemon.

· ¾ cup of goat's cheese (fresh, crumbled)

- Red pepper flakes (according to taste)

- Salt and Pepper (according to taste)

Method:

Take a large skillet and over medium heat, cook the chicken cubes in them. Season with salt and pepper and cook each side for 3 minutes each or until the chicken is cooked through. Now add the spinach, zucchini noodles and garlic powder and lemon juice to the mix.
Toss well to combine everything and continue to cook for 3 minutes or until the zucchini noodles have started to soften or the spinach leaves have started to wilt.
Once that happens, take off the heat and serve.

Serve:
Serve warm with some feta cheese and pepper flakes added on top.

Sweet n Spicy Green Pasta

Pastas are great sources of healthy proteins and carbs. With a little zucchini and baby spinach thrown into the mix, you get a delicious yet healthy meal out of it.

Nutritional Value:
- Calories: 124
- Fat: 9
- Protein:3
- Carbohydrates: 11
- Sodium: 89
- Fiber: 3

Equipment:
- Spiral slicer
- Skillet
- Blender or food processor

Ingredients:
For the Pasta:
- 4-6 organic zucchini

For the Dressing:
- 3 minced garlic cloves
- 2 chopped green onions
- ¼ cup chopped fresh parsley
- ¾ cup chopped cilantro
- 1 tablespoon raw honey
- 2 tablespoons lemon juice
- ½ cup olive oil
- 2 fresh jalapenos
- Sea salt

Method:
- Wash and create the noodles using the spiral slicer. Place all the noodles in a large bowl.
- Grill the jalapenos on a skillet. Keep turning until tender. Remove the seeds and stems. Chop.
- In a high speed blender or food processor, combine all of the ingredients except the zucchini. Blend until smooth. Add salt if necessary.

- Pour the spicy green dressing over the bowl of noodles. Mix thoroughly. Enjoy!

Top 7 Delectable Paleo Recipes

Even Paleo recipes can make use of veggettie noodles. If you have had to say bye bye to dough pasta and spaghetti, get the spiralizer going in your kitchen and try your hand at making these delectable dishes.

Egg Soup with Scallion, Ginger and Zucchini Veggettie

If you are looking for a soup which warms your heart and your soul, right down to your toes, this lovely soup will be sure to hit the right spot. Whether you have it on a cold day or not, this soup is sure to become a favorite.

Nutritional Value per serving:
· Calories: 315

· Carbohydrates: 17g

· Fat:7.5 g

· Saturated Fat: 5g

· Protein: 7g

· Fiber: 5g

Preparation Time: 10 minutes
Cooking Time: 15 minutes

This makes 1 serving. Increase measurements by multiplying them with the number of servings in mind to make more.

Ingredients
· ½ a zucchini (large, fresh, Blade A or B)

· ¾ teaspoon of canola oil

· 1 tablespoon of ginger (minced)

· 3 tablespoons of seaweed (dried)

· ½ cup of scallions (chopped)

· ¼ teaspoon of red pepper flakes

- 2 teaspoons of vinegar (sherry)

- 1 tablespoon of soy sauce (low sodium)

- 2 cups of vegetable broth

- ½ cup of water

- 1 egg (large, beaten)

- Salt and Pepper (according to taste)

Method:
Take a large saucepan and over medium heat, add the olive oil. Once it heats, add the ginger. Keep stirring and cook for 1 minute or until the ginger starts giving off an aroma. Add the vinegar, soy sauce, red pepper flakes, water and vegetable broth and allow them mixture to come to a boil.

Once this broth mixture boils, add the seaweed. Wait for a minute or two and then add the beaten egg into the broth while stirring it constantly with a spoon. Now add the scallions and zucchini noodles and season the soup with salt and pepper.

Cook the noodles in the broth for 2 minutes more. Taste your noodles to check if they are cooked to your liking before taking them off the heat.

Serve:
Serve warm with red pepper flakes added on top for extra heat.

Looking for a healthy salad? Give this lovely zucchini, sausage and broccoli salad a try. The delicious combination of these three healthy ingredients will be sure to make this healthy salad a favorite in your kitchen.

Nutritional Value per serving:

- Calories: 304

- Carbohydrates: 37g

- Fat: 14g

- Saturated Fat: 5g

- Protein: 7g

- Fiber: 5g

Preparation Time: 10 minutes
Cooking Time: 15 minutes

This makes 2 servings. Increase measurements by multiplying them with the number of servings in mind to make more.

Ingredients

- 2 zucchini (large, fresh, Blade A or B)

- 2 tablespoons of olive oil

- 2 cloves of garlic (fresh, minced)

- 1 teaspoon of red pepper flakes

- 2 sausages (spicy, chicken or Italian sausages)

- ½ cup of chicken broth

- ½ bunch of broccoli rabe

- 1 tablespoon of lemon juice (optional, fresh)

- ½ cup of Pecorino Romano cheese (freshly grated)

- Salt and Pepper (according to taste)

Method:

Wash the broccoli rabe and prepare them for the cook. Rinse and pat the leaves dry. Cut the stems and using a peeler, peel it down to the leaves.
Take a large skillet and over medium heat, add the olive oil. Slice sausages into ½ inch pieces and place them in the oil. Add oregano, salt and pepper and cook the sausages for 3 minutes per side. In the same saucepan, add the broccoli rabe you prepared and cook them evenly for 3 minutes. Season with red pepper flakes and stir cook for 1 minute.
Now add the broth and mix the broccoli rabe and the sausages together. Allow the broth to reduce completely or until the broccoli rabe has begun to wilt. Add the zucchini noodles and cook for 2 minutes or until the noodles have started to go soft.
Add the lemon juice and Pecorino Romano Cheese. Mix well and turn off the heat.

Serve:
Serve warm with red pepper flakes and flaked Pecorino Romano Cheese added on top.

Spiralized Mediterranean Chicken

Serves: 6
Ingredients

- 1 lemon

- 3 onion, chopped

- 4 tablespoons of olives, pitted and chopped

- 1 can of tomatoes

- 12 chicken thighs

- 2 pinches of black pepper

- 3 teaspoons of olive oil

- Vegetable Spaghetti

Method

- Take the lemon and using a peeler grate the peel of the fruit, making sure to say away from the white part.

- Once the zest has been removed, squeeze out the juice from the lemon.

- Mix lemon juice with the chopped onions in a slow cooker.

- Add in tomatoes as well as olives and the zest.

- Skin and wash the chicken thighs.

- Dry using paper towels and then season with salt and pepper.

- In a large skillet, add oil and let it heat over medium heat.

- Add the chicken thighs and cook on both sides until the chicken is brown all over, approximately 5 minutes on each side.

- Place the chicken thighs in the slow cooker.

- Cook on high settings for 4 hours or until done.

- Sauté your vegetable noodles spiralized using blade B in a skillet and cook until tender, season with salt and pepper.

- Serve the gravy and thighs over the noodles.
- Enjoy!

Delicious Lasagna Meal

Nutritional Value:
- Calories: 161
- Fat: 7g
- Carbohydrates: 9g
- Protein 15g
- Sodium 276 mg
- Fiber: 3g

Equipment:
- Spiral Slicer
- Baking sheets   Ingredients

For the assembly
- 6 egg whites
- 1 cup organic marinara sauce

For the filling
- 1-2 lbs free range ground turkey
- 2 cloves garlic, minced
- 1 yellow onion, chopped
- 2 teaspoons dried oregano
- 1 cup organic marinara sauceFor the Noodles:
- 1 small spaghetti squash
- 4 zucchini
- 1 Tablespoon olive oil
- 2 garlic cloves, crushed
- Dash of salt and pepper
- 2 teaspoons dried basil

Method:
- Preheat oven at 400 degrees F. Use olive oil to lightly grease 2 baking sheets and a 9×13 casserole dish with olive oil.
- Slice the spaghetti squash in half vertically. Remove the seeds, and place into a microwave safe dish with 2 inches of water.
- Microwave both halves separately (10 minutes each). Remove. Leave to cool
- Slice the zucchini into ⅛ inch lasagna noodles. Place in a single layer on the prepared baking sheets.

- Combine the olive oil, salt and pepper and dried basilin a small bowl. Brush over the noodles.
- Bake the noodles at 400 F for 10 minutes.
- Set aside to cool.
- Place the turkey in a large skillet, along with garlic, onion and oregano over medium high heat.
- Add marinara sauce when the turkey is browned, add the marinara sauce. Turn off the heat, and scrape the spaghetti squash into the skillet. Mix thoroughly.
- Use a spoon to release water from the squash by pressing down on the filling

- Top of the filling layer with eggs. Sure to crack the eggs on top of the filling and don't spread them with your hands
- Sprinkle a little more oregano and basil on the top.
- Bake for 25 minutes. Then turn on the broil for about 3 minutes. Serve and enjoy!

Sweet Potato Noodles with Shaved Asparagus and Sausage Bits

Another sweet potato recipe which can make your mouth water, this one is sure to become a favorite. Combining asparagus and sausage bits, you can get your kids to munch on this healthy meal with ease too.

Nutritional Value per serving:
· Calories: 315

· Carbohydrates: 41g

· Fat: 18g

· Saturated Fat: 5g

· Protein: 4.5g

· Fiber: 1.2g

Preparation Time: 15 minutes
Cooking Time: 15 minutes
This makes 2 servings. Increase measurements by multiplying them with the number of servings in mind to make more.

Ingredients

· 2 tablespoons of olive oil

· 2 sausage links (Italian, sweet, crumbled, de-cased)

· 1 sweet potato (fresh, large, peeled, Blade A or B)

· 1 clove of garlic (fresh, minced)

· ¼ teaspoon of red pepper flakes

· ½ cup of beef broth (low sodium)

· 2 tablespoons of parsley (fresh, chopped)

- 6 stalks of asparagus (fresh, bottoms snapped)

- Parmesan cheese (fresh, grated)

- Salt and pepper (according to taste)

Method:

Take a large skillet and over medium heat, add olive oil. Once the oil is hot, add the sausage and cook for 7 minutes or until the meat turns brown. Use the back of the spoon to crush the sausages and make it crumble into bite sized pieces. While the sausage is cooking, take a vegetable peeler and start shaving your asparagus, lengthwise. Once all the asparagus are shredded, chop the tips and set them aside.

Once the sausages are cooked, add the sweet potato noodles, red pepper flakes, garlic and season with salt and pepper. Toss the noodles to combine them properly with the sausages and spices. Then add the parsley and broth. Cook the noodles for 8 minutes or until the noodles start to soften, stirring them occasionally.

Keep an eye on the pan and when 5 minutes are up, add the shaved asparagus and cook them for the remaining 3 minutes. Once the time is up, mix everything together thoroughly and take off the heat.

Serve:
Serve warm with extra sauce and grated Parmesan cheese.

Puttanesca Veggettie

Another classic pasta dish with a vegan twist, Puttanesca veggettie is the perfect way to fulfill your spaghetti cravings without worrying about the extra carbs or calories. Eat healthy and grain free with this light, filling dish.

Nutritional Value per serving:
- Calories: 304

- Carbohydrates: 37g

- Fat: 14g

- Saturated Fat: 5g

- Protein: 7g

- Fiber: 5g

Preparation Time: 2 minutes
Cooking Time: 15 minutes

This makes 2 servings. Increase measurements by multiplying them with the number of servings in mind to make more.

Ingredients
- 1 zucchini (fresh, medium sized, Blade A or B)

- 1 tablespoon of olive oil

- 1 clove of garlic (fresh, minced)

- 1 tablespoon of capers

- 3 tablespoons of parsley (chopped)

- 1 teaspoon of red pepper (crushed)

- 2 anchovy filets

- 1 can of tomatoes (whole, peeled)

- ¼ cup of olives (Kalamata, sliced)

- Parmesan Cheese (fresh, grated)

- Salt and pepper (according to taste)

Method:

Take a large skillet and over medium heat, add olive oil. Once the oil is hot, add the anchovies and garlic. Cook them in the oil until the anchovies disintegrate into it. Crush the tomatoes with your hand and pop them into the skillet. Add the canned juices to the pan as well. Use the back of a spoon to crush the tomatoes completely.

From the anchovy tin can, use 1 teaspoon of oil and add it to the skillet along with capers, olives, parsley, salt and pepper. Allow the mixture to simmer for 10 to 15 minutes to reduce and thicken.

Once the sauce has thickened, add the zucchini noodles to them and cook for 3 minutes or until the noodles have begun to soften. Now mix everything together thoroughly and take off the heat.

Serve:

Serve warm with extra sauce and grated Parmesan cheese.

Zucchini Noodle Wrap with Feta Cheese and Avocado

A no-cook wrap which not only uses raw ingredients but is easy to whip up in a matter of minutes, this will become one of your go to snacks for sure. The recipe calls for store bought tortilla wraps but make sure they are made from 100% organic ingredients.

Nutritional Value per serving:
· Calories: 304

· Carbohydrates: 37g

· Fat: 14g

· Saturated Fat: 5g

· Protein: 7g

· Fiber: 5g

Preparation Time: 10 minutes
Cooking Time: 10 minutes

This makes 1 serving. Increase measurements by multiplying them with the number of servings in mind to make more.

Ingredients
· 1 tortilla wrap (whole grain)

· 2 tablespoons of hummus

· ¼ of an avocado (fresh, pitted, sliced)

· ½ cup of carrots (shredded finely)

· ¼ cup of black beans (pre-cooked, rinsed)

· ½ a zucchini (small, Blade A)

· 3 tablespoons of Feta cheese (crumbled)

- Salt and pepper (according to taste)

Method:

Open the tortilla wrap and spread a thin layer of hummus on it, according to your preference. Keep the hummus focused on the center and stop one inch from the edge. Start building the layers inside starting with avocado slices and season with salt and pepper, very lightly. Top with the shredded carrots and the black beans, then zucchini noodles and then add the feta cheese on top. Now roll the tortilla close and cut in half.

Serve:
Serve warm or cold with extra hummus and grated Feta cheese.

Top 7 Mouthwatering Low-Carb Recipes

It's hard to come across recipes that are not only low in carbs but also delicious. The following veggettie recipes successfully fulfill both criterion and give you a healthy dose of nutrients which can give you the boost you needed to make it through the day.

Tomato Zucchini Veggettie with Cannellini Beans, Shrimp and Roasted Artichokes

High in nutrients, this healthy low carb dish will make you feel full and happy. With great variety in texture as well, you will definitely enjoy this meal forever.

Nutritional Value per serving:
·　Calories: 304

·　Carbohydrates: 37g

·　Fat: 14g

·　Saturated Fat: 5g

·　Protein: 7g

·　Fiber: 5g

Preparation Time: 10 minutes
Cooking Time: 20 minutes

This makes 2 servings. Increase measurements by multiplying them with the number of servings in mind to make more.

Ingredients
·　1 can of artichoke hearts (cleaned, drained)

·　2 tablespoons of olive oil

·　½ teaspoon of garlic (powdered)

·　1 clove of garlic (minced)

·　¼ teaspoon of red pepper flakes

·　1/3 cup of red onions (fresh, diced)

·　1 can of tomatoes (14 oz, diced, no salt)

- 1 teaspoon of oregano (dried)

- 2 tablespoons of basil (fresh, chopped)

- 2 zucchinis (fresh, large, Blade A or B)

- 1 cup of cannellini beans (washed and dried)

- Salt and pepper (according to taste)

For the Roast Shrimp

- 8 shrimps (medium, cleaned, de-shelled and de-veined)

- ½ teaspoon of garlic powder

- Olive oil

- Salt and pepper (according to taste)

Method:

Preheat your oven to 425 degrees. Take a baking tray and line it with a baking sheet. Place the cleaned artichoke hearts on the baking sheet and drizzle some olive oil on top of them. Season with garlic powder, salt and pepper and pop them in the oven. Let them roast for 15 minutes.

Take a large skillet and on medium heat, add some olive oil to it. When the oil is hot, add the minced garlic and cook for 30 seconds or until the garlic becomes aromatic. Add the red pepper flakes and the onion and cook for 2 minutes or until the onions soften and turn transparent. Now add the tomatoes, basil, oregano and season some more with salt and pepper. Allow the mixture to simmer for 10 minutes or until the sauce starts to reduce and thicken.

In a small bowl, combine the shrimps with salt, pepper and garlic powder. Toss them well to coat them in the spices. While the sauce is reducing, take another skillet and heat up some oil on medium heat. Once the oil is hot, add the shrimps to it and cook each shrimp for 2 minutes per side or until they turn translucent then set aside.

Once the sauce has reduced, add the cannellini beans and zucchini noodles to it. Check the artichoke hearts and if they are done, take them out and add them to the sauce as well. Mix everything well and cook for 3 minutes more or until the zucchini noodles start to soften.

Serve:
Serve hot with extra sauce and the spiced shrimps added on top of each bowl.

Zucchini Noodles with Almond and Lemon Pesto

High in nutrients, this healthy low carb dish will make you feel full and happy. With great variety in texture as well, you will definitely enjoy this meal forever.

Nutritional Value per serving:
· Calories: 304

· Carbohydrates: 37g

· Fat: 14g

· Saturated Fat: 5g

· Protein: 7g

· Fiber: 5g

Preparation Time: 10 minutes
Cooking Time: 20 minutes
This makes 2 servings. Increase measurements by multiplying them with the number of servings in mind to make more.

Ingredients
· 2 zucchinis (small to medium, Blade A or B)

· 1 cup of almonds (raw)

· 1 tablespoon lemon zest

· 1 tablespoon of basil (fresh)

· 1 ½ teaspoon of garlic (minced)

· ¼ teaspoon of red pepper flakes

· ½ cup of olive oil (extra virgin)

· 1 tablespoon of lemon juice (fresh)

- Salt and pepper (according to taste)

Method:
In a food processor, blitz the basil, garlic, red pepper flakes, lemon zest and almonds and salt. Keep processing until the nuts have broken down but have not turned to powder. Turn the speed to low and slowly drizzle the olive oil into the mixture. Now add lemon juice and let it all process into a paste like consistency. Check seasoning and adjust as needed.
Take a skillet and heat some olive oil in it on medium heat. Toss the zucchini noodles and stir fry them until they are warm. Add the pesto to the noodles and toss well to mix them.

Serve:
Serve hot with extra pesto added on top of each bowl.

Fiery Sunbutter Veggettie

This amazing version of this stir fry style veggettie will give a fiery boost to your meal. If you have been missing out on stir fry, give this healthy alternative a try.

Nutritional Value per serving:
- Calories: 360

- Carbohydrates: 40g

- Fat: 20g

- Saturated Fat: 5.5g

- Protein: 14g

- Fiber: 8g

Preparation Time: 15 minutes
Cooking Time: 5 minutes

This makes 2 servings. Increase measurements by multiplying them with the number of servings in mind to make more.

Ingredients for the Base
- 2 cups of squash veggettie (small to medium, Blade A or B)

- 1 cup of sunbutter sauce

- 2 eggs (large)

- 2 teaspoons of coconut aminos

- 3 teaspoons of coconut oil

- ½ cup of onions (sliced thinly)

- 1 cup of snap peas (sliced thinly, lengthwise)

- 8 ounces of chicken thighs (pre-cooked, grilled, cubed)

Ingredients for the Sunbutter Sauce
- 2 tablespoons of lime juice (freshly squeezed)

- 1 teaspoon of garlic (minced)

- ¼ teaspoon of red pepper flakes (crushed)

- 1 tablespoon of coconut aminos

- ¼ teaspoon of ginger (powdered)

- ½ teaspoon of vinegar (rice)

- ¼ cup of sunflower butter

- ¼ cup of coconut milk

- Cayenne pepper (according to taste)

Method:

In a food processor, blitz all the ingredients for the sauce except for the coconut oil. Let them all blitz until they are well combined then stop and scrape down the sides. Add the coconut milk now and blend till you get a smooth consistency. Check seasoning and adjust as needed and set aside.

In a small bowl, combine the eggs and the coconut aminos. Now take a skillet and heat some coconut oil on low heat. Once the oil comes up to heat, add the eggs and make a crisp omelet. Cook each side for 4 minutes and place a lid on top to let the eggs cook properly. Once the omelet is ready, take it out and set aside. When cool, slice the omelet into bite sized squares.

In the same skillet, add 1 more teaspoon of coconut oil and raise the heat to medium high. Add the snap peas and onions and sauté them, stirring constantly for 2 minutes or until everything is crisp and tender.
Now add the squash veggettie, omelet bits and chicken cubes into the skillet. Stir constantly and cook for 3 minutes or until everything is hot. Add the sunbutter sauce and toss everything in it to coat them completely then take off the heat.

Serve:
Serve hot with some cilantro and a squeeze of lime juice added on top of each bowl.

Raw Veggettie Curry with Creamy Cashew Sauce

The creamy cashew sauce will make this dish a must have for you. With a good helping of raw veggettie, this curry is definitely the healthiest and most unique you can find.

Nutritional Value per serving:
·	Calories: 310

·	Carbohydrates: 10g

·	Fat: 5g

·	Saturated Fat: 2.5g

·	Protein: 14g

·	Fiber: 8g

Preparation Time: 15 minutes
Cooking Time: 5 minutes
This makes 2 servings. Increase measurements by multiplying them with the number of servings in mind to make more.

Ingredients for the Base
·	2 zucchini (medium, Blade A or B)

·	Olive oil (according to taste)

·	Sea salt (according to taste)

Ingredients for the Sunbutter Sauce

·	1 cup of cashews (pre-soaked, raw)

·	½ cup of water (fresh, filtered)

·	1 tablespoon of lime or lemon juice

·	1 teaspoon of curry powder

- ¼ teaspoon of ginger (powdered)

- ½ teaspoon of onion (powdered)

- 2 teaspoons of parsley (fresh, minced)

- 2 teaspoons of basil (fresh, minced)

- 1 teaspoon of dil (fresh minced)

- Black pepper and Sea salt (according to taste)

Method:

In a food processor, blitz all the ingredients for the sauce except for the coconut oil. Let them all blitz until they are well combined and you get a smooth sauce. If the consistency is too thin, you can add a tablespoon of water and blend again. Once you are happy with the consistency, check seasoning and adjust if needed then set aside.

In a bowl, place the veggettie and season it lightly with the olive oil, salt and pepper. Now add the sauce to the noodles and toss the noodles thoroughly to coat them with it.

Serve:

Serve cold with some cilantro added on top of each bowl.

Veggettie Pad Thai

Missing this delicious dish? Just get your hands on this recipe and you will be able to enjoy a high nutrient yet completely mouthwatering version of the traditional pad thai.

Nutritional Value per serving:
- Calories: 360

- Carbohydrates: 40g

- Fat: 20g

- Saturated Fat: 5.5g

- Protein: 14g

- Fiber: 8g

Preparation Time: 15 minutes
Cooking Time: 5 minutes

This makes 2 servings. Increase measurements by multiplying them with the number of servings in mind to make more.

Ingredients for the Pad Thai

- 2 zucchini (medium, Blade A or B)

- 1 carrot (large, Blade A or B)

- 3 pounds of chicken (boneless, precooked, skin removed)

- 1 green onion (chopped finely)

Ingredients for the Pad Thai Sauce
- 3 tablespoons of Sunbutter

- ¾ teaspoon of tamarind (paste)

- 2 tablespoons of fish sauce

- 1 teaspoon of soy sauce (can use coconut aminos instead)

- ¼ teaspoon of red chili flakes (crushed)

- ½ tablespoon of vinegar (rice)

- ¾ cup of palm sugar

- 2 ½ tablespoons of sesame oil

- 2 tablespoons of coconut oil

- 1 lime (juiced)

- ¼ teaspoon of onion (powdered)

- ¼ teaspoon of garlic (powdered)

- Black pepper and Sea salt (according to taste)

Method:

In a saucepan, heat all the ingredients for the sauce. Keep stirring the ingredients until the sugar starts to dissolve. Add a cup of water and let the sauce come to a boil before turning down the heat, allowing it to simmer and reduce gently.

Once the sauce thickens, add the zucchini and carrot noodles, green onions and the chicken cubes and toss them to coat them well with sauce. Let them cook for 3 minutes more before taking them off the heat.

Serve:

Serve hot with some crushed cashews or freshly chopped scallions added on top of each helping.

Beet Noodles with Watermelon Gazpacho

Already made with vegetables, Gazpacho is the perfect cold soup you can whip up in minutes and enjoy raw with your beet noodles.

Nutritional Value per serving:
· Calories: 101

· Carbohydrates: 18g

· Fat: 3g

· Protein: 14g

· Fiber: 3g

Preparation Time: 15 minutes
Cooking Time: 0 minutes

This makes 4 servings. Increase measurements by multiplying them with the number of servings in mind to make more.

Ingredients
· 4 cups of watermelon (de-seeded, cut into cubes)

· ½ a cucumber (seedless, peeled, diced)

· 1 tomato (large)

· 2 tablespoons of red onion (minced)

· ¼ cup of basil (fresh, chopped, can use dill or mint too)

· ¼ cup of parsley (fresh, chopped)

· 1 tablespoon of vinegar (red wine)

· 1 tablespoon of vinegar (sherry)

· 2 tablespoons of lime juice

- 1 tablespoon of olive oil (extra virgin)

- ½ a jalapeno pepper (diced)

- 2 beets (fresh, medium sized, Blade C)

- Black pepper and Sea salt (according to taste)

Method:
In a blender or food processor, combine 3 cups of watermelon, jalapeno, cucumber, parsley, basil, tomato, lime juice, the vinegars, onion and oil. Season with salt and pepper and create a puree the mixture. Once it comes to the right consistency, check seasoning and adjust if required.
Now pour the gazpacho out into a bowl and pop it into the fridge to chill.
Serve:
Serve cold with remaining watermelons and a healthy helping of the beet noodles added with each helping.

Salmon and Sesame Broccoli with Butternut Squash Veggettie

Salmon is always great when paired with vegetables and this dish allows you to take advantage of your spiralizer for this purpose.

Nutritional Value per serving:
· Calories: 400

· Carbohydrates: 20g

· Fat: 7.5g

· Protein: 16g

· Fiber: 7g

Preparation Time: 15 minutes
Cooking Time: 20 minutes

This makes 4 servings. Increase measurements by multiplying them with the number of servings in mind to make more.

Ingredients
· 4 filets of salmon (skinless, boneless)

· 2 cups of broccoli florets

· 2 butternut squashes (whole, fresh)

· Olive oil (according to taste)

· 2 tablespoons of coconut oil

· 3 teaspoons of garlic (minced)

· 2 teaspoons of ginger (minced)

· 2 teaspoons of sesame seeds (white)

· ¼ cup of coconut aminos

- 2 teaspoons of sesame oil

- 1 teaspoon of fish sauce

- 3 tablespoons of honey (raw)

- 1 teaspoon of sesame seeds (black)

Ingredients for the Marinade
- ¼ cup of coconut aminos

- 2 tablespoon of sesame oil (black)

- 3 teaspoon of sesame oil (white)

- Salt and pepper (According to taste)

Method:

Preheat your oven to 400°. Take two baking trays and line them with baking sheets before putting them aside.

In a small bowl, mix the marinade ingredients together. Take some ziplock bags and pour the marinade in the bag. Add the salmon to it and pop into the refrigerator for 10 minutes.

Now place a large pan of water on high heat allow it to boil. Once the water boils, put the broccoli in and cover the water with the lid. Let it cook for 7 minutes or until it becomes tender enough to poke with easily forked. When the broccoli is done, scoop it out and let it drain in a colander.

Now take a baking a tray and spread the veggettie noodles on it. Drizzle some olive oil and salt and pepper on it and set aside. On the other baking tray, place the salmon fillets along with their marinade. Pop the salmon into the oven and let it bake for 15 minutes or until the salmon starts to change color. When the salmon has been baking for 10 minutes, pop the veggettie noodles into the oven and let them bake for the remaining 5 minutes or longer if the noodles have not softened as yet.

Take a large saucepan and on medium heat, heat the coconut oil. Once the oil is hot, add the ginger and garlic, cooking them for 30 seconds. Now add in honey, fish sauce, sesame oil and coconut aminos into the pan. Mix well to create a thick mixture. Once the sauce thickens, add the baked noodles, broccoli and sesame seeds to the pan. Toss everything together well to combine thoroughly.

Serve:
Serve warm with the noodles and broccoli making a bed for the salmon filet. Add some sesame seeds on top as a garnish and enjoy.

7 Ultimate Weight Loss Recipes

If you are looking for recipes which promote weight loss, take a look at these. Packed with recipes which help relieve anti-oxidants and give the body vital nutrients, you will be losing weight in no time at all.

Delicious Sweet Potato Noodles

Potatoes and cheese combine in this recipe to make an unforgettable meal that is great for serving guests as well as for a quick home meal. Use a good sharp cheddar cheese to really bring out the flavor in these potato pancakes.

Nutritional information:
- Calories: 646
- Fat: 36 grams
- Carbohydrates: 79
- Protein: 13 gram

Equipment:
- Spiral Slicer

Ingredients:
- 3 green onions
- 6 tablespoons agave
- 3 tablespoons olive oil
- 3 tablespoons lemon juice
- 2 tablespoons balsamic vinegar
  - 1 pressed garlic clove
- Salt black pepper
- 3 sliced green onions
- 1/4 cup walnuts

For Pasta:
- 3 sweet potatoes

Method
- Create noodles from potatoes using spiral slicer
- Combine with agave, olive oil, lemon juice, vinegar, salt, and pepper
- Toss in the walnuts and onions
- Enjoy!

Pasta Puttanesca

If you are a pasta lover, the bold flavors of this puttanesca will hit all the right spots without the unhealthy effects of real pasta. The flavors are so mouthwatering that you won't be able to resist eating it right out of the pan.

Nutritional Value per serving:
- Calories: 300

- Carbohydrates: 13g

- Fat: 7g

- Saturated Fat: 4g

- Protein: 7g

- Fiber: 5g

Preparation Time: 30 minutes
Cooking Time: 40 minutes

This makes 4 servings. Increase measurements by multiplying them with the number of servings in mind to make more.

Ingredients
- 4 parsnips (Blade A or B)

- 1 onion (chopped)

- 3 teaspoons of garlic (grinded)

- 1 to 2 teaspoons of crushed red chili flakes

- 4 chopped fillets of anchovy (canned or fresh)

- 1 cup of tomatoes (chopped)

- 3 teaspoons of capers (chopped)

- Dash of salt

- ¼ cup of parsley

- Olive oil for frying
- Black pepper to taste

Method:

Add the olive oil to a pan or skillet and let heat on medium flame. Throw in the parsnip spaghetti and let cook, covered for 15 to 20 minutes, until done. The parsnip spaghetti should be tender when done. Remove on a plate and keep aside.
Add the chopped onions to the skillet along with garlic mince. Stir fry until onions are translucent and tender. Add in the chopped capers along with anchovies. Stir fry for a few minutes before adding in diced tomatoes and seasonings.
Allow to stir fry for a few more minutes before adding the parsnip spaghetti. Toss in the chopped parsley and pepper. Mix and remove.

Serve:
Serve warm.

Mexican Style Noodles

This recipe is so good that we could eat this every day. However Plantains are really high in carbohydrate so make sure you are watching your daily carbohydrate intake as well as the calories.

Nutritional Value per serving:
- Calories: 400

- Carbohydrates: 65g

- Fat: 10g

- Saturated Fat: 4g

- Protein: 9g

- Fiber: 5g

Preparation Time: 30 minutes
Cooking Time: 40 minutes

This makes 4 servings. Increase measurements by multiplying them with the number of servings in mind to make more.

Ingredients
- 250 grams of Steak (chopped)

- 3 teaspoons of oil

- Steak Sauce or Spices

- 2 teaspoons of Chili Powder

- 2 teaspoons of Cumin

- A dash of Cayenne

- 2 dashes of Salt

- 2 dashes of Pepper

- 3 Plantains (Blade A or B)

- 1 to 2 tablespoons of Olive Oil
- 1 large Capsicum (chopped)
- 6 Cherry Tomatoes (Sliced in half)
- Small Avocado (Diced)

Method:
Using your steak sauce or spices, marinate the chopped steak.
Heating a tablespoon of olive oil in a skillet, stir fry the steak, flipping often until done. Once done, remove and set aside on a plate.
Adding more oil to the skillet, add in the noodles and let cook, covered for 15 to 20 minutes, until done. The spaghetti should be tender when done. Once done, add in the chopped tomatoes, chopped avocado and cooked steak. Stir well and continue to cook for 5 more minutes. Mix and remove.

Serve:
Serve hot.

Stir Fry Daikon Veggettie

Enjoy this sea food, stir fry as a part of a low calorie and low carb meal, without sacrificing taste on the way. Use good quality ingredients for a delicious tasting meal.

Nutritional Value per serving:
- Calories: 200

- Carbohydrates: 16g

- Fat: 14g

- Saturated Fat: 4g

- Protein: 4g

- Fiber: 4g

Preparation Time: 10 minutes
Cooking Time: 30 minutes

This makes 4 servings. Increase measurements by multiplying them with the number of servings in mind to make more.

Ingredients
- 8 shiitake mushrooms (dried and chopped)

- 2 tablespoons of oil

- 500 grams of shrimp

- 4 green onions (chopped)

- 1 teaspoon of white pepper powder

- 1 teaspoon of salt

- 1 teaspoon of ground ginger

- 1 daikon radish (Blade A or B)

- 2 tablespoons of soy sauce

Method:

Place the mushrooms in a bowl full of water and leave to soften for about an hour. Once they are softened squeeze out excess water and chop.

Heat the oil in a skillet over medium heat. Toss in the chopped mushrooms as well as the shrimps and green onions. Mix well and toss in the seasonings. Fry the mixture until shrimps are done. Remove from the pan into a bowl.

Adding more oil to the skillet, add in the noodles and the soy sauce, mix well and let cook, covered for 15 to 20 minutes, until done. The spaghetti should be tender when done. Add in the shrimp mixture to the spaghetti. Stir well and continue to cook for 5 more minutes. Mix and remove.

Serve:

Serve hot with additional chopped green onions.

Spicy Fries

These spicy fries are ideal for the times when you are in mood for something crunchy to snack on.

Nutritional Value per serving:
·   Calories: 250

·   Carbohydrates: 50g

·   Fat: 0.5g

·   Saturated Fat: 0.2g

·   Protein: 4.5g

·   Fiber: 30g

Preparation Time: 10 minutes
Cooking Time: 30 minutes

This makes 2 servings. Increase measurements by multiplying them with the number of servings in mind to make more.

Ingredients
·   1 medium to large jicama (Blade A or B)

·   2 tablespoons of olive oil

·   2 dashes of salt

·   3 teaspoons of onion powder

·   2 teaspoons of cayenne pepper or paprika

·   2 teaspoons of chili powder

Method:

Before you start putting the recipe together, you want to preheat your oven for 12 minutes at 400 degrees. Once you have spiralized the jicama, if you like, you can make them smaller to match the size of real fries.

Now, spread the noodles on a baking sheet, taking care to not place them too close together. Pour olive oil evenly over the fries and sprinkle with the seasonings. Toss to coat well. Place the baking tray in oven and let it bake for 12 to 15 minutes, before turning them over and continuing to bake for another 15 minutes.

Serve:

Serve straight from the oven, dividing in two to three servings.

Mint and Cucumber Noodles with Ginger Vinaigrette

This salad is great for hot summer days as it is easy to prepare and really refreshing to eat.

Nutritional Value per serving:
·   Calories: 260

·   Carbohydrates: 9.9g

·   Fat: 25g

·   Saturated Fat: 3.4g

·   Protein: 18g

·   Fiber: 3g

Preparation Time: 10 minutes
Cooking Time: 0 minutes

This makes 2 servings. Increase measurements by multiplying them with the number of servings in mind to make more.

Ingredients
·   9 teaspoons of olive oil

·   5 Tablespoons of fresh lemon juice

·   1 teaspoon soy sauce

·   Half a teaspoon of grated ginger

·   Black Pepper to taste

·   1 teaspoon chili flakes

·   1 large cucumber (Blade C)

·   1 handful fresh mint

·   1 green onion (chopped)

- 6 teaspoons of sesame seeds

Method:
Combine olive oil, lemon juice, ginger, soy sauce, black pepper and chili flakes in a bowl and mix well. Spiralize the cucumber and add chopped mint and chopped green onion to it. Pour the dressing over the cucumber, mint and onion mixture. Toss to coat well.

Serve:
Sprinkle sesame seeds over the salad and eat immediately.

Italian Meatball Veggettie Soup

This soup can be prepared overnight in a slow cooker. You will wake up to delicious aroma of soup in the morning. You can also prepare it in the morning, leave it in the slow cooker for 6 hours while you take care of your tasks and then come back to a steaming bowl of hearty soup.

Nutritional Value per serving:
· Calories: 126

· Carbohydrates: 3g

· Fat: 6g

· Saturated Fat: 3.4g

· Protein: 18g

· Fiber: 3g

Preparation Time: 30 minutes
Cooking Time: 6 to 7 hours

This makes 4 servings. Increase measurements by multiplying them with the number of servings in mind to make more.

Ingredients
· 900 ml of chicken or beef Stock

· 1 Zucchini (Blade A or B)

· 2 medium Celery (Chopped)

· 1 Onion (chopped)

· 1 large Carrot (Chopped)

· 1 Tomato (chopped)

· ½ tablespoon of Garlic powder

· 700 grams of minced beef

- ½ Cup of grated Parmesan Cheese
- 4 teaspoons of minced Garlic
- 1 medium egg
- 6 Tablespoons of Parsley (Chopped)
- ½ a tablespoon of Salt
- ½ a tablespoon of Onion Powder
- 1 teaspoon of Italian Seasoning
- 1 teaspoon of Oregano
- ½ teaspoon of Pepper

Method:

Switch your slow cooker on, keeping it on the lowest setting.

Pour in the beef stock and add in the chopped vegetables including zucchini, onions, celery, tomato and carrots. Sprinkle garlic powder over the vegetables, mix and place cover.

Add minced beef to a bowl and add in Parmesan and egg. Mix well and add in minced garlic, salt, onion powder, pepper, oregano and Italian seasoning. Mix once again. Now, take a small amount of mixture in between your palms form into a ball. Set aside on a greased tray and continue forming the remaining mixture into meatballs.

Pour oil into a wok or skillet and place over medium heat. Add the meatballs into hot oil and let it brown all over. Cook all of the meatballs, leave slightly underdone. Uncover the slow cooker and add in the meatballs. Place the cover and let cook for another 6 hours.

Serve:
Serve hot.

Top 7 Holiday Recipes

Get into the holiday spirit with these seven low calorie holiday dishes. Now you can easily counter the calories and enjoy nutritious meals which can let you enjoy the festive occasion without any calorie guilt.

Sausages Wrapped in Sweet Potato (Halloween)

These sausages are easy to prepare and when done they look like little master pieces that would leave your guests awestruck. No one needs to know how little work went in to preparing these. That can be our little secret.

Nutritional Value per serving:
· Calories: 112

· Carbohydrates: 5.9g

· Fat: 8g

· Saturated Fat: 1.4g

· Protein: 3.6g

· Fiber: 1g

Preparation Time: 20 minutes
Cooking Time: 20 minutes

This makes 16 servings. Increase measurements by multiplying them with the number of servings in mind to make more.

Ingredients
· 2 sweet potatoes (Blade A or B)

· 6 teaspoons of ghee

· 1 teaspoon salt

· 8 medium sized hot dogs (split in halves)

· 32 sunflower seeds

Method:

Before you start putting the recipe together, you want to preheat your oven for 12 minutes at 400 degrees.

Take a baking tray and spread aluminum foil over it, folding around the corners to cover it completely. Spread about a teaspoon or two of melted ghee over the tray to grease it. Place the spiralized sweet potato in a large bowl and add in the remaining melted ghee as well as salt. Mix well.

Take hot dog halves and start wrapping the sweet potato strands all around them. Make sure that the strands of sweet potato don't overlap. The hot dog half should be covered completely. Place the covered hot dogs on the greased baking tray. These hot dogs are supposed to resemble mummies so the sweet potato strands act as bandages.

Allow a small gap on the hot dog that should act as a face. Push in two sunflower seeds in to the face to act as eyes. Place the tray in to the oven and bake for twenty minutes or until crisp and golden brown.

Serve:

Serve standing upright on a plate with a pool of ketchup around them to act as blood.

Apple Veggettie Funnel Cake

These funnel cakes are great when enjoyed as breakfast with a hot beverage and they are really simple to make as well.

Nutritional Value per serving:
·   Calories: 265

·   Carbohydrates: 50g

·   Fat: 4g

·   Saturated Fat: 1.2g

·   Protein: 8.6g

·   Fiber: 1.3g

Preparation Time: 20 minutes
Cooking Time: 30 minutes

This makes 8 servings. Increase measurements by multiplying them with the number of servings in mind to make more.

Ingredients
·   3 large eggs

·   4 tablespoons of sugar

·   1 cup of Hot Apple Cider

·   250 ml of milk

·   3 teaspoons of vanilla

·   3 cups flour

·   2 dashes of salt

·   3 teaspoon of cinnamon

·   2 dashes of allspice

- 2 teaspoons of baking powder
- 4 tablespoons of powdered sugar
- 3 teaspoons of ground cinnamon

Method:

In a small bowl, beat together eggs and sugar. Add in vanilla and continue beating until creamy. Pour in the Hot Apple Cider and continue beating for a minute. Add in the milk next and beat some more.

In another medium sized bowl, mix together flour and salt. Add in the ground cinnamon as well as allspice. Mix well and add in the baking powder. Now pour in the wet ingredients into the dry ingredients. Mix well until no lumps remain.

Heat a skillet filled with oil. When the oil is well heated, add the batter into squeeze bottles and pour it into the hot oil, making small sized cakes. Brown the funnel cake on both sides before removing from the oil and placing it on a plate. Continue cooking until the entire mixture is done.

Serve:

In another bowl, mix together the 3 teaspoons of ground cinnamon with powdered sugar. Use this mixture to dust the cakes before serving. Serve hot.

Butternut Squash Noodles with Roasted Pecans and Cranberry and Orange Sauce

This is the ideal recipe for a holiday. It is warm and filling and is guaranteed to give you the warm afterglow that is true of holiday meals.

Nutritional Value per serving:
- Calories: 255

- Carbohydrates: 15g

- Fat: 14g

- Saturated Fat: 4.2g

- Protein: 6g

- Fiber: 4g

Preparation Time: 10 minutes

Cooking Time: 30 minutes

This makes 5 servings. Increase measurements by multiplying them with the number of servings in mind to make more.

Ingredients
- 4 tablespoons of maple syrup

- 4 tablespoons of water

- 4 tablespoons of cranberry juice

- 1 cup of cranberries

- 1 teaspoon of grated orange zest

- 4 tablespoons of orange juice

- Salt to taste

- Pepper to taste

- · 1 large butternut squash (Blade A or B)
- · Olive oil
- · 8 tablespoons of pecans
- · Honey

Method:

Before you start putting the recipe together, you want to preheat your oven for 12 minutes at 400 degrees.

Take a large saucepan and place it over medium to high heat. Add in the maple syrup, water, cranberry juice, zest, orange juice as well as salt and pepper into the pan. Place a lid on the pan and allow it to come to a boil. Once the mixture starts boiling, reduce the flame and let it simmer for 15 to 20 minutes, stirring frequently until the sauce reaches desired consistency. Pour the sauce into a bowl and set aside.

Place the noodles on the baking tray and pour olive oil over it and toss to coat. Season the noodles with salt and pepper. Place the baking sheet into the oven and bake for ten minutes or until done. When done, remove and add to a small bowl and set aside. In the same baking tray, spread pecans and drizzle it with honey. Let it bake for 3 to 5 minutes. Pour the sauce over the noodles and mix well.

Serve:

Divide the noodles in to serving bowls and top with roasted pecans.

Sweet Potato Veggettie with Buffalo Style Chicken

This is a very simplc but delicious recipe that can be whipped up in minutes and can help serve guests and family while earning your praises as well.

Nutritional Value per serving:
- Calories: 350

- Carbohydrates: 20g

- Fat: 16g

- Saturated Fat: 6.2g

- Protein: 10g

- Fiber: 6g

Preparation Time: 10 minutes

Cooking Time: 30 minutes

This makes 6 servings. Increase measurements by multiplying them with the number of servings in mind to make more.

Ingredients
- 1 Cup Cream

- 1 heaped tablespoon of Butter

- 4 teaspoons of Starch

- 2 tablespoons of hot sauce

- Salt to taste

- Pepper to taste

- 2 dashes of Garlic Powder

- ½ teaspoon of Chili Powder

- 500 grams of Chicken

- 3 medium sized Sweet Potato (Blade A or B)
- 3 Tablespoons of oil

Method:

Take a medium sized saucepan and add in the cream and butter. Mix well. Add in the starch and hot sauce, next. Now add the seasonings including salt, pepper and garlic powder. Mix well and lastly whisk in chili powder. Place over medium heat and continue stirring until it is thick. In a skillet, heat oil and fry chicken till done. Set it aside. In the same skillet, add the noodles and cook till tender.

Serve:

Serve the noodles in bowls and top with chicken and cream sauce. Enjoy!

Beet Pear Noodles with Pistachio and Bacon Dressing

Beet serves as a great addition to salads. However when prepared as a part of this recipe, it creates a melody of flavors that will leave you reaching for more.

Nutritional Value per serving:
· Calories: 380

· Carbohydrates: 18g

· Fat: 12g

· Saturated Fat: 8.2g

· Protein: 8g

· Fiber: 4g

Preparation Time: 20 minutes

Cooking Time: 30 minutes

This makes 6 servings. Increase measurements by multiplying them with the number of servings in mind to make more.

Ingredients
· 1 English muffin (halved)

· 4 teaspoons of olive oil

· 1 tablespoon of parsley (chopped)

· Salt to taste

· Pepper to taste

· 2 ounces of goat cheese

· 2 slices bacon

· 1 Anjou pear (Blade A or B)

- 1 beet (Blade A or B)
- 15 roasted pistachios (deshelled)
- 1 heaping teaspoon of honey
- ½ teaspoon of Dijon mustard
- Pepper to taste
- 1 teaspoon of red wine vinegar

Method:

Preheat your oven for 12 minutes at 400 degrees.

Add the muffin to a food processor and grind till it forms breadcrumbs.

Take a skillet and place it over low to medium heat. Add in about a teaspoon of oil and fry the breadcrumbs until they are brown and toasted. Remove and transfer to a bowl. Add in the chopped parsley as well as salt and pepper into the bowl. .

Taking the goat cheese, roll it in the breadcrumb mixture until well coated. Coat a baking tray with oil and place the cheese on the tray. Take another baking tray and coat it with oil. Place the beet noodles on this tray. Place both baking trays into an oven and bake for 7 to 10 minutes.

In a skillet, crisp fry the bacon and set aside the grease in a bowl while placing the bacon on a tissue towel to absorb grease from it. Add pistachios, honey, vinegar, pepper and mustard into the food processor and grind into a paste. Mix in about a tablespoon of bacon grease. Add the beet noodles and pear noodles into a large bowl. Pour the pistachio mixture on top of it and mix to coat well.

Serve:

Divide the noodles into individual bowls and top with goat cheese. Crumble the fried and dried Bacon over the bowls.

Brussels Sprout and Apple Salad with Almonds and Sweet Hot Mustard Sauce

Who says you have to give up on fruit when you spiralize? With this tasty salad, you can try your spiralizer out on fruits and you will definitely enjoy what you manage to make!

Nutritional Value per serving:
· 	Calories: 184

· 	Carbohydrates: 20g

· 	Fat: 11g

· 	Saturated Fat: 1g

· 	Protein: 4g

· 	Fiber: 4g

Preparation Time: 20 minutes

Cooking Time: 15 minutes

This makes 6 servings. Increase measurements by multiplying them with the number of servings in mind to make more.

Ingredients to Make the Sweet Hot Mustard
· 	2 tablespoons of Dijon mustard

· 	1 tablespoon of mustard (whole grain)

· 	¾ tablespoons of vinegar (apple cider)

· 	2 tablespoons of honey

· 	½ teaspoon of sriracha sauce

Ingredients for the Salad
· 	4 shallots (fresh, thinly sliced)

· 	1 tablespoon of vinegar (sherry)

- 3.5 tablespoons of olive oil (extra virgin)
- 1 pound of Brussels sprouts
- ½ almonds (thinly sliced)
- 2 apples (red Gala, Blade C)

Method:

In a bowl, combine all the ingredients you need to make the hot mustard. Use a whisk to mix everything together thoroughly. Once the sauce is to your liking set aside.

Take a skillet and place it over medium heat. Add in half a teaspoon of oil, shallots, some salt and pepper. Now place a lid upon it and let them cook for 3 minutes or until they have started to caramelize. Take the caramelized shallots out and add them to the mustard mixture with a dash of the sherry vinegar, a tablespoon of olive oil and some more salt and pepper. Mix and then set aside. In the same skillet, add the remaining olive oil and Brussels sprouts. Season well with salt and pepper before covering the pan and cooking them for 8 minutes or until the Brussels sprouts have turned brown and become tender. Once the Brussel sprouts are ready, pop them into the mustard mixture. Add your almonds and apple noodles and toss everything together to coat them well.

Serve:

Serve warm with some extra almond slivers added on top of the salad.

Cucumber Noodle Salad in Greek Style

Who says you have to give up on fruit when you spiralize? With this tasty salad, you can try your spiralizer out on fruits and you will definitely enjoy what you manage to make!

Nutritional Value per serving:
· Calories: 225

· Carbohydrates: 16g

· Fat: 16g

· Protein: 7g

· Fiber: 4g

Preparation Time: 5 minutes

Cooking Time: 0 minutes

This makes 1 serving. Increase measurements by multiplying them with the number of servings in mind to make more.

Ingredients for the Salad
· ½ of a cucumber (English, seedless, Blade A or B)

· ¼ of a bell pepper (green, chopped)

· 1/3 cup of tomatoes (grape tomatoes, halved)

· 5 olives (Kalamata, pitted)

· 1 tablespoon of red onions (fresh, sliced)

· ½ a lemon (fresh)

· 1 oz of Feta Cheese (thickly sliced)

· ½ tablespoon of olive oil (extra virgin)

· ½ teaspoon of oregano leaves (minced)

Method:

In a bowl, combine all the olives, cucumbers, tomatoes, bell peppers and red onions. Drizzle lemon juice, half of the olive oil and season with salt and pepper. Toss the salad to coat it well.

Serve:

Serve as is with some thick feta cheese slices added on top of the salad.

Top 7 Storage Tips

Now that you know how to whip up these amazing dishes using the spiralizer, you need to know how to store them too. It's really not that complicated and here are 7 tips you can follow for storage purposes.

1.   Store Fresh

Always store veggettie which is fresh and right off the spiralizer since vegetables start to go bad with exposure to air. If you wait to store any leftovers after you are done cooking, you will have to use them up quickly too since they will not last as long as fresh ones.

2.   Airtight Containers

Airtight containers are your best friends. These are perfect for sealing the veggettie and also help the noodles retain their flavor and crispness. This is extremely useful since it helps keep your noodles fresh even if you cook them after a day or two.

3.   Zip Lock Bags

These will be your second best friend. Use these in conjunction with the airtight containers. If you don't have airtight containers, you can place your noodles inside the zip lock bag and then place them inside the container.

While they don't keep the noodles as good as the airtight containers, they are still good for when you want to use the noodles the next day.

4. Label Them

Make sure to put a label with the kind of fruit or vegetable you made the veggettie out of and the date you made it on. This ensures you use up all the noodles you have in your fridge, reducing over-hoarding and wastage as well as helping you remember which noodles are made from which ingredient.

5. Freezing Veggettie

Freezing can be a viable option but only for certain kinds of veggettie. Sweet potato and squash veggettie respond nicely to it. They can appear limp but when cooking them, they tend to cook faster and better as compared to their usual state.

6. Storing in the Fridge

Zucchini and cucumber veggettie lasts better when stored in the fridge. Their high water content means the whole noodle freezes but it turns to mush when it is thawed and does not have much taste or freshness to them.

7. Keep an Eye on Shelf Life

Now don't forget about your veggettie once you have popped them in the fridge and freezer. Ideally, squash and zucchini noodles can last for 4 or 5 days. Cucumber is only good for 2 or 3 days because the high water content makes them go soggy faster. Sweet potato, if frozen, can last you longer but should be consumed within the week.

Conclusion

Well, here we are at the end of the eBook. We hope that with the help of all the information contained within, you not only fell in love with your spiralizer machine but also got to enjoy eating veggettie.

Looking to help you lead a healthier lifestyle, we hope this eBook was successful in this purpose. Now at the start, you may fall and stumble and make a few mistakes but with the help of the information provided here, you will be able to conquer those problems and cook efficiently and effectively.

Once you are confident enough, you will be able to cook like a pro in no time at all!

Good Luck!

Also, Don't Forget To Pick this Bestselling Spiralizer Cookbook By Ali Maffucci

Inspiralized: Turn Vegetables into Healthy, Creative, Satisfying Meals

Get it Here Now >> http://www.amazon.com/Inspiralized-Vegetables-Healthy-Creative-Satisfying-ebook/dp/B00O02AMLQ

Enjoy

If you enjoyed the recipes in this book, please take the time to share your thoughts and post a positive review with 5 star rating on Amazon, it would encourage us and make us serve you better. It'll be greatly appreciated!

If you have any question or anything at all you want to know about this program, you can hit me up via mail thru **Laurahill@gmail.com** I am always there to help you.

Other Health And Fitness Bestselling Books

DASH Diet Cookbook: A 7-Day-7lbs Dash Diet Plan: 37 Quick and Easy Dash Diet Recipes to help lower your blood pressure, Lose weight and Feel Great! Get it Here Now>> http://www.amazon.com/dp/B00X1I5TZE

DASH Diet: DASH Diet Ultimate Beginners Guide: 37 Quick and Easy DASH Diet Recipes to Help you Lose Weight Fast, Lower Blood Pressure and Feel Great!
DASH Diet Slow Cooker Cookbook: A 7-Day-7lbs Dash Diet Plan: 37 Delicious Dash Diet Slow Cooker Recipes to help lower your blood pressure, Lose weight and Feel Great!

The 20/20 Diet: Turn Your Weight Loss Vision Into Reality Download it Here>> http://www.amazon.com/20-Diet-Weight-Vision-Reality-ebook/dp/B00QMPH9W4

Spiralizer Slow-Cooker Cookbook:**Ultimate Beginners guide to Vegetable Pasta Spiralizer: Top Spiralizer Slowcooker Recipes For Weight loss, Gluten-free, Low Carb, Low Calorie Recipes, Paleo Recipes… etc**
Get it Here Now>> http://www.amazon.com/Spiralizer-Slow-Cooker-Cookbook-Slowcooker-Gluten-free-ebook/dp/B00VD7N9WK/

It Starts with Good food: It Starts with Good food Cookbook: 57 Quick & Easy Paleo Recipes For your Nutritional Reset Get it Here Now>> http://www.amazon.com/Starts-Good-food-Cookbook-Nutritional-ebook/dp/B00USURU5U

10-Day Green Smoothie Cleanse: 35 Yummy Green Smoothies Recipes to Help Lose 15lbs in 10 Days! Get it Here Now>> http://www.amazon.com/10-Day-Green-Smoothie-Cleanse-Smoothies-ebook/dp/B00U1U3JTS

My Burn the Belly Plan Diet Recipes: Recipes to Help you Burn Belly Fat Fast!

Get it Here Now>> http://www.amazon.com/Burn-Belly-Plan-Diet-Recipes-ebook/dp/B00UZFZGQ8

10 Day Detox Diet Cookbook: 50 All-New Recipes to Help you Burn the Fat, Lose weight Fast and Boost your Metabolism For Busy Mom
Get it Here Now>> http://www.amazon.com/Day-Detox-Diet-Cookbook-Metabolism-ebook/dp/B00UDGH7A2

Spiralizer Cookbook: 50 All-New Delicious & Healthy Veggetti Spiral Recipes to Help You Lose Weight, Lower Blood Pressure Using Vegetable Pasta Spiralizer- for Paderno, Veggetti Shredders!
Get it Here Now>> http://www.amazon.com/Spiralizer-Cookbook-Delicious-Vegetable-Spiralizer--ebook/dp/B00TKHB33W